The First Christmas at the Piano

12 Favorite Carols Arranged For Piano Solo

by Samuel Wilson

No. 207

Associated Music Publishers, Inc.

DISTRIBUTED BY

HAL•LEONARD®
CORPORATION

7777 W. BLUEMOUND RD. P.O. BOX 13819 MILWAUKEE, WI 53213

T0050919

CONTENTS

Title   Page

Away in a Manger 2

First Noel, The 11

Hark! The Herald Angels Sing 12

I Heard the Bells on Christmas Day 3

I Wish You a Merry Christmas 6

It Came upon a Midnight Clear 4

Joy to the World 7

O Come, All Ye Faithful 8

O Little Town of Bethlehem 5

Silent Night 1

We Three Kings 10

What Child Is This? 9

Silent Night

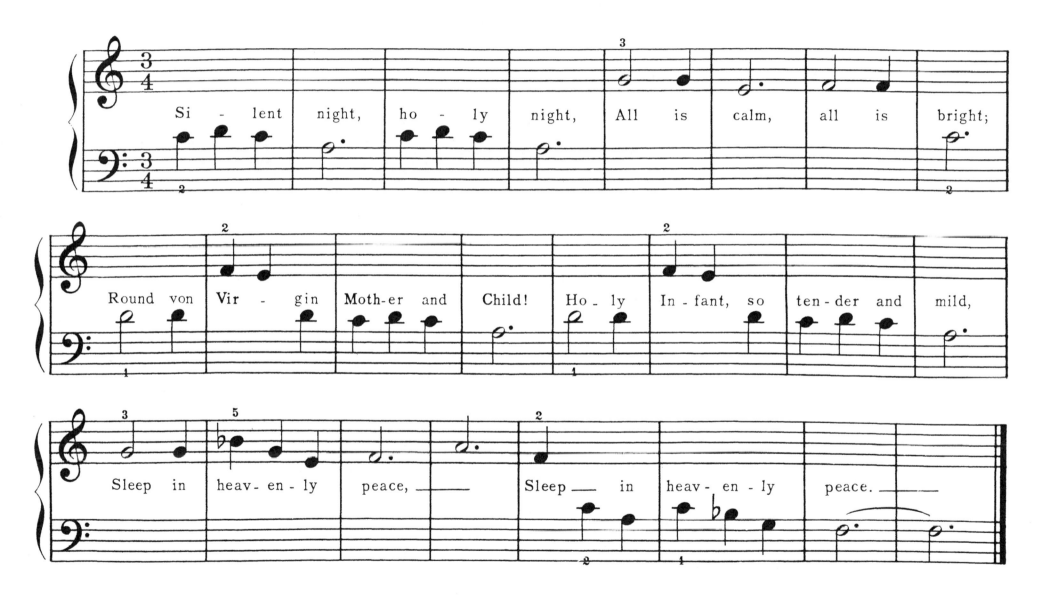

Away in a Manger

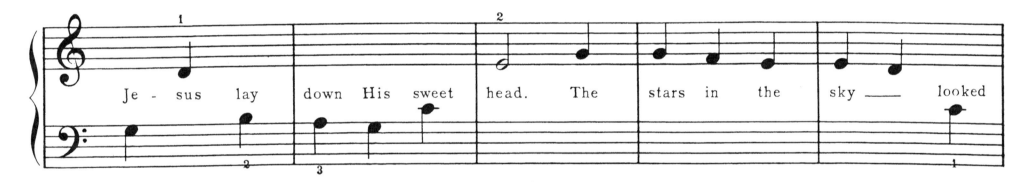

I Heard the Bells on Christmas Day

I heard the bells on Christ-mas day Their old fa-mil-iar

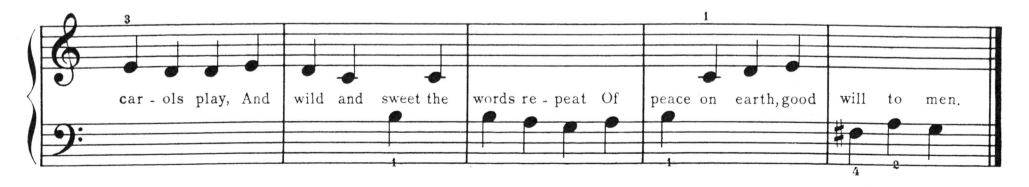

car-ols play, And wild and sweet the words re-peat Of peace on earth, good will to men.

It Came upon the Midnight Clear

It came up-on — the mid-night clear, That glo-ri-ous song — of old, — From an-gels bend-ing

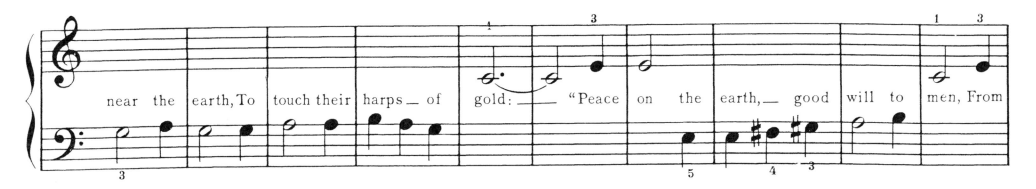

near the earth, To touch their harps — of gold: — "Peace on the earth, — good will to men, From

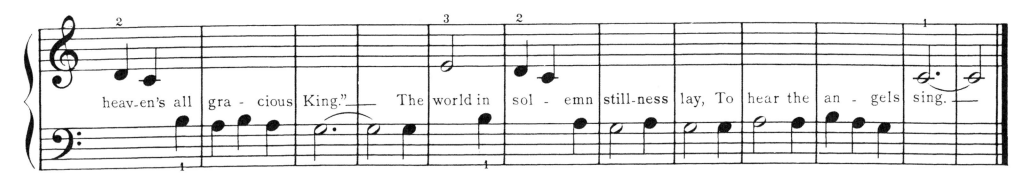

heav-en's all gra-cious King." — The world in sol-emn still-ness lay, To hear the an-gels sing. —

O Little Town of Bethlehem

I Wish You a Merry Christmas

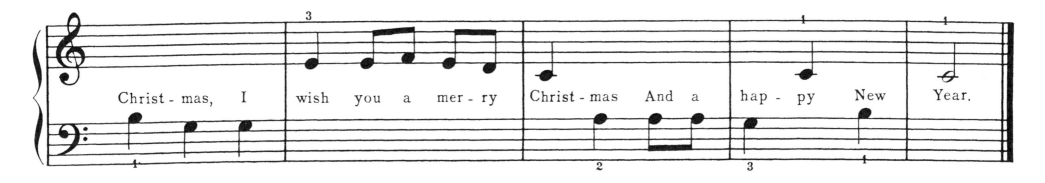

Joy to the World

O Come, All Ye Faithful

What Child Is This?

We Three Kings

The First Noël

Hark! The Herald Angels Sing